# Getting Started with AI: Artificial Intelligence

## Introduction

Welcome to "Getting Started with AI: Artificial Intelligence." In this comprehensive ebook, we will embark on a journey through the fascinating world of Artificial Intelligence (AI). AI has become an integral part of our lives, influencing industries, transforming businesses, and impacting the way we interact with technology. This ebook is designed to provide you with a solid foundation in AI, whether you are a complete beginner or someone looking to expand their knowledge in this rapidly evolving field. We will explore the basics of AI, its applications, and its implications for the future.

By the end of this ebook, you will have a clear understanding of what AI is, how it works, and how you can get started on your own AI journey. So, let's dive in and discover the incredible world of Artificial Intelligence.

## Table of Contents:



## Chapter 1: Introduction to AI

### 1.1 What is AI?

Artificial Intelligence, often abbreviated as AI, is a transformative field in computer science that strives to create intelligent machines capable of mimicking human cognitive functions. These cognitive functions include learning, reasoning, problem-solving, perception, language understanding, and even the ability to interact with the environment. AI seeks to enable machines to perform tasks that typically require human intelligence, and it has grown to encompass a wide range of techniques and applications.

At its core, AI is about building algorithms and systems that can process data, make decisions, and adapt to changing circumstances. These algorithms are designed to learn from experience, recognize patterns in data, and make predictions or decisions based on that knowledge. AI systems can be highly specialized, focusing on solving specific problems, or more general, aiming to replicate human-like intelligence.

The key characteristics that distinguish AI from traditional computer programs are:

Learning: AI systems can learn from data, improving their performance over time. They adapt and refine their strategies as they receive more information.

Reasoning: AI systems can analyze information, draw conclusions, and make decisions based on their understanding of the data and their programmed logic.

Problem-Solving: AI can be used to tackle complex problems that involve a high degree of uncertainty or require processing vast amounts of data.

Perception: AI systems can interpret and understand sensory inputs, such as images, audio, and text, to extract meaningful information.

Language Understanding: AI can process and generate human language, enabling natural language interactions with machines.

Interaction: AI can interact with the environment, whether it's through controlling physical robots or virtual agents in digital spaces.

## 1.2 A Brief History of AI

The history of AI is a captivating journey through innovation, challenges, and breakthroughs. It spans several decades and is marked by significant milestones that have shaped the field into what it is today.

- 1950s: The Birth of AI
  The term "Artificial Intelligence" was coined in 1956 during a Dartmouth College conference where leading researchers gathered to explore the possibilities of creating machines that could think like humans. This event is considered the birth of AI as a field of study.
- 1960s: Early Progress
  In the 1960s, AI research was marked by the development of rule-based expert systems. These systems used logical rules to simulate human expertise in specific domains.

- 1970s: AI Winter
  The 1970s saw a period known as the "AI Winter," marked by dwindling interest and funding in AI research due to unrealized expectations and technical limitations. Progress was slower than anticipated.
- 1980s: Expert Systems
  The 1980s saw a resurgence of interest in AI, driven by advancements in expert systems. These systems, designed to mimic human decision-making, found applications in fields like medicine and finance.
- 1990s: Machine Learning Resurgence
  Machine learning, a subfield of AI focused on building algorithms that can learn from data, gained prominence in the 1990s. This decade witnessed significant progress in areas like natural language processing and computer vision.
- 2000s: Big Data and Deep Learning
  The 2000s marked the era of big data, where the proliferation of digital information allowed AI systems to learn from vast datasets. Deep learning, a subfield of machine learning, made remarkable strides, revolutionizing areas like image and speech recognition.
- 2010s: AI Goes Mainstream
  The 2010s witnessed AI becoming an integral part of daily life. Virtual assistants like Siri and Alexa, recommendation systems on streaming platforms, and autonomous vehicles all became prominent examples of AI in action.
- 2020s: Ongoing Advancements
  As of my last knowledge update in September 2021, AI continued to advance rapidly. Deep learning models like GPT-3 and reinforcement learning algorithms were making headlines, and AI was being applied across industries, from healthcare to finance and beyond.

## 1.3 Types of AI

AI is a diverse field, and AI systems can be categorized into various types based on their capabilities and scope. Understanding these types is essential in grasping the breadth of AI applications. Here are some common categories:

- Narrow AI (Weak AI): Narrow AI refers to AI systems designed for specific tasks or domains. These systems excel in their designated area but lack general intelligence. Examples include virtual personal assistants like Siri and image recognition software.

- General AI (Strong AI): General AI, often depicted in science fiction, is an AI system with human-like intelligence and the ability to understand, learn, and perform any intellectual task that a human can. We have not yet achieved true general AI.
- Machine Learning: Machine learning is a subset of AI that focuses on building algorithms and models that can learn from data. It includes techniques like supervised learning, unsupervised learning, and reinforcement learning.
- Supervised Learning: In supervised learning, AI models are trained on labeled data, which means the algorithm is provided with examples where the correct answers are known. It learns to make predictions or classifications based on this labeled data.
- Unsupervised Learning: Unsupervised learning involves training AI models on unlabeled data, encouraging them to find patterns, clusters, or structures within the data on their own.
- Reinforcement Learning: Reinforcement learning is a type of machine learning where agents learn to make decisions by interacting with an environment. They receive rewards or penalties based on their actions, allowing them to learn optimal strategies.
- Deep Learning: Deep learning is a subfield of machine learning that involves neural networks with multiple layers. These deep neural networks have been exceptionally successful in tasks like image and speech recognition.
- Natural Language Processing (NLP): NLP focuses on enabling machines to understand, interpret, and generate human language. It is crucial for applications like chatbots, language translation, and sentiment analysis.

## 1.4 Why AI Matters

The significance of AI extends far beyond its technical capabilities. It has become a transformative force across various industries and holds the potential to shape the future in profound ways. Here are some compelling reasons why AI matters:

- Efficiency and Automation: AI can automate repetitive tasks, freeing up human resources for more creative and strategic endeavors. In industries like manufacturing, logistics, and customer service, automation can lead to increased efficiency and cost savings.

- Data Analysis and Insights: AI excels at processing and analyzing vast amounts of data quickly. This capability is invaluable in fields like healthcare, where AI can assist in diagnosing diseases based on medical images or predicting patient outcomes.
- Personalization: AI powers recommendation systems that provide personalized content, products, and services. This enhances user experiences on platforms like Netflix, Amazon, and social media.
- Innovation: AI fuels innovation by enabling the development of novel applications and solutions. Startups and established companies alike are harnessing AI to create new products and services.
- Sustainability: AI can contribute to sustainability efforts by optimizing resource allocation, predicting environmental trends, and improving energy efficiency.
- Healthcare: AI has the potential to revolutionize healthcare by assisting in early disease detection, drug discovery, and treatment optimization.
- Autonomous Systems: AI is at the heart of autonomous vehicles, drones, and robots, enabling them to navigate and make decisions

# Chapter 2: Machine Learning Fundamentals

## 2.1 Understanding Machine Learning

Machine Learning (ML) is a subset of Artificial Intelligence (AI) that focuses on developing algorithms and models that can learn from data. Unlike traditional computer programs that rely on explicit instructions, machine learning systems improve their performance by discovering patterns, making predictions, and optimizing their behavior through experience.

At the core of machine learning is the idea that algorithms can analyze and learn from data to make informed decisions or predictions. This ability to learn and adapt is what sets machine learning apart from traditional programming. Here are some key concepts and components of machine learning:

- Data: Data is the foundation of machine learning. ML algorithms require data to learn patterns, relationships, and trends. This data can take various forms, including text, numbers, images, and more.
- Features: Features are the specific characteristics or attributes within the data that the ML algorithm uses to make

predictions. For example, in a machine learning model for predicting house prices, features could include the number of bedrooms, square footage, location, and more.

- Labels: In supervised learning, which is one of the main branches of machine learning, data is often labeled. This means that each example in the training dataset is paired with a corresponding "label" or "target," which represents the correct answer or outcome. For instance, in a spam email classifier, each email is labeled as either "spam" or "not spam."
- Training Data: The training data is a subset of the overall dataset that is used to teach the machine learning model. The model learns from this data by identifying patterns and relationships between features and labels.
- Model: The model is the heart of a machine learning system. It's a mathematical representation or algorithm that learns to map input data (features) to output predictions. The model's parameters are adjusted during training to minimize the difference between its predictions and the actual labels.
- Algorithm: The algorithm is the set of rules and procedures that guide the learning process of the model. Different machine learning algorithms are suited to different types of problems and data.
- Training: Training is the process of feeding the training data to the machine learning model and adjusting its parameters so that it can make accurate predictions. The goal of training is to minimize the model's prediction errors.
- Testing and Evaluation: After training, the model's performance is assessed using a separate dataset called the testing dataset. This helps measure how well the model generalizes to new, unseen data. Evaluation metrics, such as accuracy, precision, recall, and F1-score, are used to assess the model's performance.

Machine learning can be categorized into several subfields, each with its own set of techniques and applications. Some of the main subfields include:

- Supervised Learning: In supervised learning, the model is trained on a dataset where each example is paired with a known label or target. The goal is for the model to learn a mapping from input features to output labels so that it can make accurate predictions on new, unseen data. Common algorithms used in supervised learning include Linear

Regression, Decision Trees, Random Forests, Support Vector Machines (SVM), and Neural Networks.

- Unsupervised Learning: Unsupervised learning deals with datasets that lack labeled targets. Instead, the algorithm seeks to discover patterns, structures, or clusters within the data. Common techniques in unsupervised learning include Clustering (e.g., K-Means), Dimensionality Reduction (e.g., Principal Component Analysis), and Association Rule Mining.
- Reinforcement Learning: Reinforcement learning is concerned with training agents to make sequential decisions in an environment to maximize a cumulative reward. Agents learn by interacting with the environment and receiving feedback in the form of rewards or penalties. Popular reinforcement learning algorithms include Q-Learning, Deep Q-Networks (DQN), and Policy Gradient methods.
- Deep Learning: Deep learning is a subset of machine learning that focuses on neural networks with multiple layers (deep neural networks). Deep learning has achieved remarkable success in various domains, including computer vision, natural language processing, and speech recognition. Convolutional Neural Networks (CNNs) are commonly used for image-related tasks, while Recurrent Neural Networks (RNNs) and Transformers are popular for sequence data and language-related tasks.

## 2.2 Supervised Learning

Supervised learning is one of the fundamental branches of machine learning. In supervised learning, the algorithm is provided with a dataset that includes both input features and corresponding output labels or targets. The goal of the algorithm is to learn a mapping from the input features to the output labels so that it can make accurate predictions on new, unseen data.

Here are the key components and concepts of supervised learning:

- Training Data: The training dataset consists of examples, where each example includes a set of input features and the corresponding correct output label. For instance, in a spam email classifier, the training data would consist of emails along with labels indicating whether each email is "spam" or "not spam."
- Features: Features are the input variables or attributes that the model uses to make predictions. These can be

numerical, categorical, or even text-based. The choice of features is crucial in determining the model's performance.

- Labels: Labels are the output values that the model aims to predict. In binary classification, there are typically two labels: positive and negative. In multi-class classification, there are more than two possible labels.
- Model: The supervised learning model is a mathematical representation or algorithm that learns to make predictions based on the input features. The model's parameters are adjusted during training to minimize the difference between its predictions and the actual labels.
- Algorithm: The choice of the supervised learning algorithm depends on the problem type (classification or regression) and the nature of the data. Common algorithms for classification tasks include Logistic Regression, Decision Trees, Random Forests, Support Vector Machines (SVM), and Neural Networks.
- Training: During the training phase, the algorithm is exposed to the training data. It uses this data to adjust its internal parameters in such a way that it can map the input features to the correct output labels as accurately as possible. This adjustment process is often referred to as "learning."
- Testing and Evaluation: After training, the model's performance is assessed using a separate dataset called the testing dataset. This dataset contains examples that the model has not seen during training. Evaluation metrics, such as accuracy, precision, recall, and F1-score, are used to measure the model's ability to generalize to new data.

Supervised learning can be further categorized into two main types:

- Classification: In classification tasks, the goal is to assign input examples to one of several predefined classes or categories. For example, classifying emails as spam or not spam, identifying images of cats and dogs, or detecting diseases based on medical images are all classification problems.
- Regression: In regression tasks, the goal is to predict a continuous numerical value or quantity. This could involve predicting housing prices based on features like square footage and location, forecasting stock prices, or estimating the time it takes to complete a task.

## 2.3 Unsupervised Learning

Unsupervised learning is a branch of machine learning where the algorithm is presented with a dataset that lacks labeled output targets. In other words, the algorithm is not provided with explicit information about the correct answers or categories for each example in the data. Instead, unsupervised learning algorithms are tasked with discovering patterns, structures, or relationships within the data.

Key concepts and techniques in unsupervised learning include:

- Clustering: Clustering algorithms aim to group similar data points together into clusters or categories. Common clustering algorithms include K-Means Clustering and Hierarchical Clustering. Applications of clustering include customer segmentation, image segmentation, and document clustering.
- Dimensionality Reduction: Dimensionality reduction techniques seek to reduce the number of features or variables in a dataset while preserving its essential characteristics. Principal Component Analysis (PCA) is a widely used dimensionality reduction method. It is valuable for reducing the complexity of data and visualizing high-dimensional datasets.
- Anomaly Detection: Anomaly detection algorithms identify unusual or anomalous data points that deviate significantly from the expected or typical patterns in the data. Anomalies can represent errors, fraud, or rare events. Techniques like Isolation Forests and One-Class SVMs are used for anomaly detection.
- Density Estimation: Density estimation methods estimate the probability density function of the data distribution. Kernel Density Estimation (KDE) and Gaussian Mixture Models (GMMs) are examples of density estimation techniques. These methods can be useful in statistical analysis and data modeling.
- Association Rule Mining: Association rule mining identifies relationships, associations, or patterns in transactional data. It is commonly used in market basket analysis, where the goal is to discover items that are frequently purchased together. The Apriori algorithm is a classic example of an association rule mining technique.

Unsupervised learning is particularly useful in scenarios where the data is unstructured, and the goal is to gain insights, discover hidden structures, or preprocess data for further analysis. While there are no explicit output labels, the patterns and structures uncovered by unsupervised learning algorithms can be valuable for making informed decisions.

One notable application of unsupervised learning is in natural language processing (NLP), where techniques like topic modeling and word embeddings (e.g., Word2Vec and GloVe) are used to uncover semantic relationships between words and documents.

## 2.4 Reinforcement Learning

Reinforcement Learning (RL) is a branch of machine learning that focuses on training agents to make sequences of decisions in an environment to maximize a cumulative reward. RL is inspired by behavioral psychology, where learning is driven by the consequences of actions.

In reinforcement learning, an agent interacts with an environment, takes actions, receives feedback in the form of rewards or penalties, and learns to improve its decision-making process over time. The primary components of reinforcement learning are as follows:

- Agent: The agent is the learner or decision-maker in the RL system. It interacts with the environment and selects actions to achieve specific goals.
- Environment: The environment represents the external system with which the agent interacts. It includes all elements, entities, and factors that influence the agent's actions and outcomes.
- State: A state is a representation of the current situation or configuration of the environment. It contains information that is relevant to the agent's decision-making process.
- Action: Actions are the choices made by the agent that affect the state of the environment. The agent selects actions based on its current state and the goal it aims to achieve.
- Reward: Rewards are numerical values provided by the environment to indicate the desirability of the agent's actions. Positive rewards indicate good actions, while negative rewards (penalties) signal undesirable actions. The agent's objective is to maximize its cumulative reward over time.
- Policy: The policy is a strategy or set of rules that the agent uses to map states to actions. It defines the agent's behavior and decision-making process.
- Value Function: The value function is a mathematical function that estimates the expected cumulative reward that an agent can achieve from a given state or state-action pair.

It helps the agent evaluate the desirability of different states and actions.

Reinforcement learning scenarios often involve an agent learning to make a sequence of decisions that lead to long-term rewards. This is known as the "credit assignment problem," where the agent must determine which actions contributed to a positive or negative outcome even when the consequences are delayed.

Reinforcement learning algorithms can be categorized into model-free and model-based approaches:

- Model-Free RL: Model-free RL algorithms focus on learning a policy or value function directly from interactions with the environment. Common algorithms in this category include Q-Learning, SARSA, and Deep Q-Networks (DQN).
- Model-Based RL: Model-based RL algorithms aim to build a model of the environment, including its dynamics and transitions. These algorithms use the learned model to plan and make decisions. Model-based RL can be particularly useful in situations where exploration in the real environment is expensive or risky.

Reinforcement learning has found success in a wide range of applications, including robotics, game playing (e.g., AlphaGo), autonomous vehicles, recommendation systems, and healthcare. It excels in scenarios where the optimal decision-making strategy may not be known in advance, and the agent must learn from its interactions with the environment.

## 2.5 Deep Learning

Deep Learning (DL) is a subfield of machine learning that focuses on artificial neural networks with multiple layers, known as deep neural networks. Deep learning has garnered significant attention and achieved remarkable success in various domains, including computer vision, natural language processing (NLP), speech recognition, and reinforcement learning.

Key concepts and components of deep learning include:

- Neural Networks: Neural networks are computational models inspired by the structure and function of biological neurons in the human brain. They consist of interconnected nodes or artificial neurons organized into layers.
- Layers: A neural network typically comprises multiple layers, including an input layer, one or more hidden layers, and an output layer. Each layer consists of multiple neurons or nodes that process and transform the input data.

- Activation Functions: Activation functions introduce non-linearity into the neural network, enabling it to learn complex patterns and relationships within the data. Common activation functions include the sigmoid function, hyperbolic tangent (tanh), and rectified linear unit (ReLU).
- Weights and Biases: Neural networks learn by adjusting the weights and biases associated with each connection between neurons. These adjustments occur during training and are guided by an optimization algorithm.
- Feedforward Propagation: Feedforward propagation is the process by which input data is passed through the neural network's layers to produce an output prediction. This prediction is then compared to the actual target or label to compute a loss or error.
- Backpropagation: Backpropagation is the core algorithm used for training neural networks. It calculates the gradients of the loss with respect to the network's weights and biases and updates them to minimize the loss.
- Deep Learning Architectures: Deep learning encompasses various architectures tailored to specific tasks. Convolutional Neural Networks (CNNs) are designed for image-related tasks, Recurrent Neural Networks (RNNs) excel in sequential data analysis, and Transformers are used for NLP and language-related tasks.
- Training Data: Deep learning models require large amounts of labeled training data to learn complex patterns. The availability of extensive datasets has contributed to the success of deep learning.
- Pretrained Models: Transfer learning is a common practice in deep learning, where pretrained models are fine-tuned on specific tasks. This approach leverages the knowledge learned from one task to improve performance on another.
- Optimization Algorithms: Various optimization algorithms, such as stochastic gradient descent (SGD), Adam, and RMSprop

# Chapter 3: AI in Practice

Artificial Intelligence (AI) is not just a concept confined to research labs and science fiction anymore; it's a transformative force that's reshaping numerous industries and impacting our daily lives. In this chapter, we will delve into the real-world applications of AI, exploring how AI technologies are being used across various sectors, from healthcare and finance to transportation and entertainment. We'll also examine the challenges and opportunities that come with the widespread adoption of AI.

# 3.1 Real-world Applications of AI

AI is not a distant future technology; it's here and now, permeating almost every aspect of our lives. Let's take a closer look at how AI is being applied in practice across different domains:

### 3.1.1 Healthcare

### 3.1.1.1 Medical Imaging

One of the most significant breakthroughs in healthcare is the use of AI in medical imaging. AI algorithms can analyze medical images such as X-rays, CT scans, and MRIs with incredible precision. This has led to earlier and more accurate diagnoses of conditions like cancer, fractures, and neurological disorders. For example, deep learning models can detect abnormalities in mammograms, helping radiologists identify breast cancer at an early stage.

### 3.1.1.2 Drug Discovery and Development

AI is revolutionizing the drug discovery process. It can analyze vast datasets to identify potential drug candidates and predict their effectiveness. AI-powered drug discovery accelerates the development of new medications, reducing costs and increasing the chances of success. Pharmaceutical companies are increasingly using AI to optimize clinical trials and streamline the drug development pipeline.

### 3.1.1.3 Personalized Medicine

AI enables the development of personalized treatment plans based on an individual's genetic makeup and medical history. This approach, known as precision medicine, ensures that treatments are tailored to the patient's unique characteristics, increasing the likelihood of successful outcomes and minimizing side effects. AI-powered genomics and medical AI platforms are at the forefront of this revolution.

### 3.1.1.4 Virtual Health Assistants

Virtual health assistants and chatbots equipped with AI can provide healthcare information, answer medical queries, and even schedule doctor appointments. They play a crucial role in telemedicine, making healthcare services more accessible and efficient, especially in remote areas.

## 3.1.2 Finance

### 3.1.2.1 Algorithmic Trading

AI-driven algorithms are used extensively in financial markets for high-frequency trading. These algorithms analyze market data, news, and social media sentiment to make split-second trading decisions. They can identify arbitrage opportunities and manage portfolios with precision.

### 3.1.2.2 Fraud Detection

Banks and financial institutions leverage AI to detect fraudulent activities. Machine learning models can identify unusual patterns and anomalies in transactions, helping prevent credit card fraud, identity theft, and other financial crimes.

### 3.1.2.3 Credit Scoring

Traditional credit scoring models are being augmented or replaced by AI-driven models. These models consider a broader range of data, including non-traditional sources such as social media activity and online behavior, to assess creditworthiness. This approach can extend credit access to underserved populations.

### 3.1.2.4 Robo-Advisors

Robo-advisors use AI algorithms to provide automated investment advice and portfolio management. They offer cost-effective, data-driven investment strategies tailored to individual goals and risk tolerance.

## 3.1.3 Transportation

### 3.1.3.1 Autonomous Vehicles

Self-driving cars and autonomous vehicles rely on AI for perception, decision-making, and navigation. AI algorithms process sensor data from cameras, LiDAR, radar, and GPS to safely navigate and make real-time driving decisions.

### 3.1.3.2 Traffic Management

AI plays a critical role in optimizing traffic flow and reducing congestion in smart cities. Traffic management systems use AI to analyze data from traffic cameras and sensors, adjust traffic signals in real-time, and predict traffic patterns.

### 3.1.3.3 Ride-sharing and Delivery Services

Ride-sharing platforms and delivery services use AI for route optimization, pricing, and demand forecasting. These algorithms ensure efficient and cost-effective transportation services.

## 3.1.4 Entertainment

### 3.1.4.1 Content Recommendation

Streaming platforms like Netflix and Spotify use AI algorithms to recommend content to users based on their viewing or listening history. These recommendation systems increase user engagement and content consumption.

### 3.1.4.2 Content Creation

AI can generate content, including art, music, and writing. Generative models like GANs (Generative Adversarial Networks) can create realistic images and videos, while AI-powered chatbots can generate human-like text.

### 3.1.4.3 Video Games

AI is integral to modern video games, enabling non-player characters (NPCs) to exhibit lifelike behavior and adapt to player actions. Procedural generation techniques also use AI to create vast and dynamic game worlds.

# 3.1.5 Manufacturing

### 3.1.5.1 Quality Control

Manufacturers use computer vision and machine learning to inspect products for defects. AI-powered systems can identify imperfections in real-time, reducing manufacturing errors and improving product quality.

### 3.1.5.2 Predictive Maintenance

AI-driven predictive maintenance models analyze sensor data from machinery to predict when equipment is likely to fail. This enables proactive maintenance, minimizing downtime and costly repairs.

### 3.1.5.3 Supply Chain Optimization

AI optimizes supply chain operations by forecasting demand, optimizing inventory, and managing logistics. This results in cost savings and improved efficiency.

# 3.1.6 Marketing and Advertising

### 3.1.6.1 Customer Segmentation

AI analyzes customer data to segment audiences based on demographics, behavior, and preferences. Marketers can then tailor their campaigns to specific customer segments for higher conversion rates.

### 3.1.6.2 Content Personalization

AI-driven content recommendation engines personalize website content and email marketing based on user behavior. This increases user engagement and conversion rates.

### 3.1.6.3 Ad Targeting*

Machine learning algorithms optimize ad targeting by predicting which ads are most likely to resonate with specific audiences. This results in more effective and efficient advertising campaigns.

# 3.2 AI in Healthcare

AI has had a profound impact on healthcare, transforming how we diagnose, treat, and manage medical conditions. Here are some key applications of AI in healthcare:

### 3.2.1 Medical Imaging

AI-powered image analysis tools can detect abnormalities in medical images, such as X-rays, CT scans, and MRIs, with remarkable accuracy. These tools assist radiologists in diagnosing conditions like cancer, fractures, and neurological disorders.

### 3.2.2 Disease Diagnosis and Risk Prediction

Machine learning models can analyze patient data, including electronic health records (EHRs) and genetic information, to assist in disease diagnosis and risk prediction. AI algorithms can identify early warning signs of diseases and help healthcare providers make more informed decisions.

### 3.2.3 Drug Discovery and Development

AI accelerates drug discovery by analyzing vast datasets and simulating drug interactions. It identifies potential drug candidates and predicts their effectiveness, reducing the time and cost of bringing new medications to market.

### 3.2.4 Personalized Treatment Plans

Precision medicine leverages AI to develop personalized treatment plans based on an individual's genetic profile and medical

# Chapter 4: AI Ethics and Challenges

In this chapter, we delve into the ethical considerations and challenges associated with the development and deployment of Artificial Intelligence (AI). As AI technologies continue to advance and become increasingly integrated into our daily lives, it's essential to address the ethical implications and potential pitfalls that accompany this progress.

## 4.1 Understanding AI Ethics

AI ethics encompasses the principles, guidelines, and moral considerations that govern the development, deployment, and use of artificial intelligence technologies. It seeks to ensure that AI systems are designed and employed in ways that are fair, transparent, accountable, and aligned with human values.

Ethical considerations in AI can be broadly categorized into several key areas:

### 4.1.1 Fairness and Bias

One of the foremost ethical concerns in AI is fairness. AI systems can inherit biases present in their training data or the algorithms themselves. These biases can lead to discriminatory outcomes, reinforcing existing inequalities in society. AI fairness aims to mitigate bias and ensure that AI systems treat all individuals and groups equitably.

### 4.1.2 Transparency and Accountability

AI systems often operate as "black boxes," making it challenging to understand their decision-making processes. Transparency and accountability in AI require that developers and organizations provide clear explanations of how AI systems work and take responsibility for their actions. This is especially important in critical applications like healthcare and criminal justice.

### 4.1.3 Privacy and Data Security

AI systems rely on vast amounts of data, raising concerns about privacy and data security. Ethical AI practices involve safeguarding sensitive data, obtaining informed consent for data usage, and ensuring that AI applications comply with privacy regulations such as GDPR (General Data Protection Regulation).

### 4.1.4 Autonomy and Control

As AI becomes more autonomous, questions arise about who controls AI systems and to what extent. Ethical considerations include defining the boundaries of AI decision-making and ensuring that humans retain control over AI systems, particularly in high-stakes scenarios like autonomous vehicles and healthcare.

### 4.1.5 Accountability and Liability

Determining responsibility and liability for AI-generated outcomes can be complex. Ethical AI practices involve establishing clear lines of accountability, especially when AI systems are involved in accidents or harm.

### 4.1.6 Bias and Discrimination

Bias in AI systems can perpetuate discrimination against certain groups. Ethical AI requires proactive measures to identify and address bias, including diverse and representative training data, fairness-aware algorithms, and ongoing monitoring.

## 4.2 The Challenges of AI Ethics

Addressing AI ethics is not without its challenges. Here are some of the key obstacles and dilemmas that arise when striving for ethical AI:

### 4.2.1 Bias Mitigation

Mitigating bias in AI systems is a complex task. Bias can be introduced at various stages, from data collection and preprocessing to algorithm design and decision-making. Detecting and rectifying bias requires a combination of technical and ethical considerations.

### 4.2.2 Data Privacy

Balancing the need for data to train AI systems with individual privacy rights is challenging. Collecting and using personal data must be done responsibly and in compliance with data protection laws. Additionally, anonymization techniques may not always guarantee complete privacy.

### 4.2.3 Transparency and Explainability

AI models, especially deep learning models, can be highly complex and difficult to interpret. Ensuring transparency and explainability in AI systems is crucial for building trust and understanding how decisions are made. Striking the right balance between accuracy and interpretability is an ongoing challenge.

### 4.2.4 Accountability

Determining who is accountable for AI-generated decisions or actions can be challenging. In cases where AI systems make errors or cause harm, defining liability and responsibility is complex and may require legal and regulatory frameworks to evolve.

### 4.2.5 Ethical Dilemmas in Autonomous AI

Autonomous AI systems, such as self-driving cars and drones, raise ethical dilemmas regarding their decision-making in critical situations. These systems must navigate complex moral choices, such as prioritizing passenger safety over pedestrian safety or vice versa.

### 4.2.6 Regulation and Governance

Developing effective regulations and governance frameworks for AI is a multifaceted challenge. Striking the right balance between fostering innovation and ensuring responsible AI usage is an ongoing debate in the AI ethics community.

## 4.3 Ethical Frameworks and Guidelines

To navigate the ethical landscape of AI, various organizations, researchers, and institutions have proposed ethical frameworks and guidelines. These frameworks provide guidance for developers, policymakers, and organizations to ensure that AI technologies are designed and used in ethically responsible ways. Here are some notable ethical frameworks:

### 4.3.1 The Five Principles of AI Ethics (IBM)

IBM's AI ethics framework revolves around five core principles:

- Fairness: AI systems should avoid bias and ensure fairness in their treatment of all individuals and groups.
- Transparency: The operation of AI systems should be transparent and explainable.
- Accountability: Organizations should take responsibility for the outcomes of AI systems.

- Robustness: AI systems should be designed to withstand adversarial attacks and unforeseen circumstances.
- Privacy: Protecting the privacy of individuals' data is paramount.

**4.3.2 The AI Ethics Guidelines (EU)**

The European Commission has proposed guidelines for trustworthy AI, emphasizing the following principles:

- Human Agency and Oversight: AI should empower individuals and respect human autonomy.
- Technical Robustness and Safety: AI systems should be secure, reliable, and free from biases.
- Privacy and Data Governance: Data protection and privacy rights should be upheld.
- Transparency: AI systems should be explainable and decisions should be understandable.
- Accountability: Clear roles and responsibilities should be defined for AI systems.

**4.3.3 The Asilomar AI Principles (Future of Life Institute)**

The Asilomar AI Principles, endorsed by AI researchers and experts, cover a wide range of ethical considerations:

- Research Goal: AI should be used for the benefit of all humanity.
- Research Funding: Funding should prioritize AI research that aligns with ethical principles.
- Avoiding Harm: AI systems should not harm humanity or concentrate power unduly.
- Long-Term Safety: Research should focus on ensuring the safety of AI over the long term.
- Technical Leadership: AI researchers should take a leadership role in shaping AI's impact on society.
- Cooperative Orientation: AI development should involve cooperation and collaboration among researchers and institutions.

# 4.4 Ensuring Ethical AI Development

Developing AI ethically requires a multifaceted approach that involves various stakeholders. Here are some key strategies for ensuring ethical AI development:

**4.4.1 Diverse and Inclusive Teams**

Building diverse teams that include individuals from different backgrounds, experiences, and perspectives is crucial. Diverse teams are more likely to identify and address bias and ethical issues in AI development.

### 4.4.2 Ethical Training and Education

Training AI developers, engineers, and data scientists in ethical considerations is essential. Ethical education should be an integral part of AI curricula, ensuring that future practitioners are equipped to make ethical decisions.

### 4.4.3 Ethical Impact Assessment

Conducting ethical impact assessments for AI projects can help identify potential risks and ethical concerns early in the development process. These assessments should be part of standard practice.

### 4.4.4 Continuous Monitoring and Auditing

AI systems should undergo regular monitoring and auditing to identify bias, discrimination.

# Chapter 5: Advanced AI Techniques

In this chapter, we explore advanced AI techniques that go beyond the fundamentals covered earlier in this book. These techniques represent the cutting edge of AI research and application, pushing the boundaries of what is possible in the field of artificial intelligence. We'll delve into topics such as deep reinforcement learning, generative adversarial networks, natural language processing, and more.

## 5.1 Deep Reinforcement Learning

Deep reinforcement learning (DRL) is a subfield of AI that combines reinforcement learning with deep learning techniques. It has gained significant attention and success in various applications, including robotics, autonomous systems, and game playing. At its core, DRL involves training agents to make sequences of decisions in an environment to maximize cumulative rewards.

### 5.1.1 Key Concepts in Deep Reinforcement Learning

- Agent: The agent is the learner or decision-maker in the DRL system. It interacts with the environment, takes actions, and receives feedback in the form of rewards or penalties.
- Environment: The environment represents the external system with which the agent interacts. It includes all elements, entities, and factors that influence the agent's actions and outcomes.
- State: A state is a representation of the current situation or configuration of the environment. It contains information that is relevant to the agent's decision-making process.

- Action: Actions are the choices made by the agent that affect the state of the environment. The agent selects actions based on its current state and the goal it aims to achieve.
- Reward: Rewards are numerical values provided by the environment to indicate the desirability of the agent's actions. Positive rewards indicate good actions, while negative rewards (penalties) signal undesirable actions. The agent's objective is to maximize its cumulative reward over time.
- Policy: The policy is a strategy or set of rules that the agent uses to map states to actions. It defines the agent's behavior and decision-making process.
- Value Function: The value function is a mathematical function that estimates the expected cumulative reward that an agent can achieve from a given state or state-action pair. It helps the agent evaluate the desirability of different states and actions.

### 5.1.2 DRL Algorithms

Several DRL algorithms have been developed, each with its strengths and applications:

- Q-Learning: Q-Learning is a classic DRL algorithm that aims to learn the optimal action-value function, denoted as $Q(s, a)$, which estimates the expected cumulative reward of taking action "a" in state "s." It's the basis for many DRL approaches.
- Deep Q-Networks (DQN): DQN combines Q-Learning with deep neural networks. It uses a deep neural network to approximate the Q-function, allowing it to handle high-dimensional state spaces, making it suitable for tasks like playing video games.
- Policy Gradient Methods: Policy gradient methods directly learn the agent's policy by optimizing its parameters to maximize expected rewards. These methods, such as REINFORCE and TRPO, are particularly effective for problems with continuous action spaces.
- Actor-Critic Methods: Actor-critic methods combine elements of policy-based and value-based approaches. They use an actor network to learn the policy and a critic network to estimate the value function. Algorithms like A3C and DDPG fall into this category.

### 5.1.3 Applications of Deep Reinforcement Learning

Deep reinforcement learning has demonstrated remarkable success in various domains:

- Game Playing: DRL algorithms have achieved superhuman performance in games like Chess, Go, and video games. AlphaGo, developed by DeepMind, famously defeated the world champion Go player.
- Robotics: DRL is used in robotics for tasks like robot control, manipulation, and navigation. Robots can learn to perform complex actions in real-world environments through reinforcement learning.
- Autonomous Vehicles: Self-driving cars and autonomous drones employ DRL for decision-making and navigation. DRL enables these vehicles to adapt to changing road conditions and environments.
- Healthcare: DRL is applied to optimize treatment plans and drug discovery. It can help determine the best treatment options for patients and identify promising drug candidates.

## 5.2 Generative Adversarial Networks (GANs)

Generative Adversarial Networks (GANs) are a groundbreaking class of deep learning models introduced by Ian Goodfellow and his colleagues in 2014. GANs consist of two neural networks, a generator, and a discriminator, that are trained together through a competitive process.

### 5.2.1 Key Concepts in GANs

- Generator: The generator network takes random noise or a latent vector as input and generates data samples. Its goal is to produce data that is indistinguishable from real data.
- Discriminator: The discriminator network evaluates data samples and tries to distinguish between real data and fake data generated by the generator. Its goal is to correctly identify the source of the data.
- Adversarial Training: GANs use adversarial training, where the generator and discriminator are in a constant battle. The generator aims to produce data that fools the discriminator, while the discriminator aims to become better at distinguishing real from fake data.
- Nash Equilibrium: In an ideal scenario, GANs reach a Nash equilibrium where the generator produces data that is indistinguishable from real data, and the discriminator can't improve its performance further.

### 5.2.2 Applications of GANs

GANs have a wide range of applications across different domains:

- Image Generation: GANs can generate realistic images of faces, animals, objects, and scenes. They are used in art, graphic design, and even in creating realistic video game environments.
- Image-to-Image Translation: GANs can transform images from one domain to another. For example, they can convert black-and-white photos to color or translate satellite images to maps.
- Style Transfer: GANs can change the artistic style of an image while preserving its content. This is used in art and design to create unique visual effects.
- Super-Resolution: GANs can enhance the resolution of images, making them sharper and more detailed. This has applications in medical imaging, surveillance, and photography.
- Data Augmentation: GANs can generate synthetic data that can be used to augment training datasets for machine learning models. This is especially useful when real data is scarce.

## 5.3 Natural Language Processing (NLP)

Natural Language Processing (NLP) is a branch of AI that focuses on the interaction between computers and human language. It enables computers to understand, interpret, and generate human language, facilitating communication and information extraction.

### 5.3.1 Key Concepts in NLP

- Tokenization: Tokenization is the process of breaking text into individual words or tokens. It's the first step in many NLP tasks.
- Part-of-Speech Tagging: This involves tagging each word in a sentence with its grammatical category, such as noun, verb, adjective, etc.
- Named Entity Recognition (NER): NER identifies and classifies named entities in text, such as names of people, places, organizations, and dates.
- Sentiment Analysis: Sentiment analysis determines the sentiment or emotional tone of a piece of text, whether it's positive, negative, or neutral.
- **Machine Translation

(MT): Machine translation is the process of automatically translating text from one language to another. Prominent examples of machine translation systems include Google Translate and DeepL.

- Topic Modeling: Topic modeling techniques, such as Latent Dirichlet Allocation (LDA), aim to discover hidden topics or themes within a collection of documents.
- Named Entity Recognition: Named Entity Recognition (NER) is the process of identifying and classifying named entities (such as names of people, places, organizations, and dates) in text.
- Text Generation: Text generation models, including recurrent neural networks (RNNs) and transformer-based models like GPT-3, can generate human-like text. These models are used in chatbots, content generation, and creative writing.
- Question Answering: Question Answering models can extract answers from text in response to natural language questions. They are used in applications like virtual assistants and search engines.

### 5.3.2 Challenges in Natural Language Processing

NLP presents several challenges, including:

- Ambiguity: Natural language is inherently ambiguous, with words and phrases often having multiple meanings depending on context. Resolving this ambiguity is a significant challenge in NLP.
- Context Understanding: Understanding the context of a conversation or document is crucial for accurate language processing. Context can span sentences or even entire paragraphs.
- Lack of Annotated Data: Many NLP tasks require large annotated datasets for training, and creating such datasets can be time-consuming and expensive.
- Multilingual Processing: Handling multiple languages and language variations is a complex task in NLP, requiring specialized models and resources.
- Ethical Concerns: NLP also raises ethical concerns, such as bias in language models, misinformation spread, and privacy issues related to language data collection.

# 5.4 Computer Vision

Computer vision is an AI field that enables machines to interpret and understand visual information from the world, including images and videos. It has diverse applications ranging from facial recognition and autonomous vehicles to medical image analysis and augmented reality.

### 5.4.1 Key Concepts in Computer Vision

- Image Classification: Image classification involves assigning a label or category to an image. Convolutional Neural Networks (CNNs) have revolutionized image classification, achieving human-level accuracy on tasks like ImageNet classification.
- Object Detection: Object detection identifies and localizes objects within an image. Popular object detection models include Faster R-CNN and YOLO (You Only Look Once).
- Image Segmentation: Image segmentation divides an image into regions or segments, typically to identify objects' boundaries within the image.
- Face Recognition: Face recognition systems can identify and verify individuals by analyzing facial features. They are used for security, access control, and entertainment.
- Optical Character Recognition (OCR): OCR technology converts printed or handwritten text within images into machine-readable text. It's used in document scanning and digitization.
- Pose Estimation: Pose estimation determines the positions and orientations of objects or body parts in an image. It has applications in augmented reality and robotics.

### 5.4.2 Advanced Computer Vision Techniques

- Convolutional Neural Networks (CNNs): CNNs are the foundation of modern computer vision. They use convolutional layers to automatically learn features from images, making them highly effective for tasks like image classification and object detection.
- Transfer Learning: Transfer learning involves using pre-trained CNN models on large datasets like ImageNet and fine-tuning them for specific tasks. This technique significantly reduces the need for large annotated datasets.
- Semantic Segmentation: Semantic segmentation assigns a class label to every pixel in an image, enabling precise object delineation. Models like U-Net and DeepLab are used for this task.
- Generative Models for Images: Generative models like Variational Autoencoders (VAEs) and Generative Adversarial Networks (GANs) can generate realistic images.

StyleGAN, for example, is known for generating high-quality synthetic faces.
- 3D Computer Vision: 3D computer vision deals with understanding the 3D structure of objects and scenes from 2D images. This is crucial for applications like augmented reality and autonomous navigation.

### 5.4.3 Applications of Computer Vision

Computer vision finds applications in various domains:
- Autonomous Vehicles: Computer vision is essential for self-driving cars and drones, enabling them to perceive and navigate the environment.
- Medical Imaging: Computer vision aids in medical diagnosis by analyzing X-rays, MRIs, and CT scans. It can detect diseases and anomalies.
- Retail: Computer vision is used for inventory management, cashier-less stores, and customer analytics through facial recognition.
- Augmented Reality (AR): AR applications overlay digital information onto the real world. This is used in gaming, navigation, and training simulations.
- Security and Surveillance: Computer vision systems monitor and analyze video feeds for security purposes, such as detecting intruders or identifying license plates.

# 5.5 Reinforcement Learning in Robotics

Reinforcement learning (RL) has made significant strides in the field of robotics, enabling robots to learn complex tasks and adapt to dynamic environments. RL-based robots learn from trial and error, interacting with their surroundings to achieve specific goals.

### 5.5.1 Challenges in RL for Robotics
- Sample Efficiency: Training RL-based robots can be data-intensive and time-consuming. Improving sample efficiency is crucial to reducing training time.
- Safety: Ensuring the safety of RL-based robots, especially in real-world scenarios, is a top priority. Robots need to learn without causing harm to themselves or others.
- Transfer Learning: Transferring knowledge from simulation to the real world is a challenge. RL models often require adaptation when transitioning from simulated environments to physical ones.

- Multi-Agent Systems: Coordinating multiple RL-based robots in a team or swarm presents complex challenges in terms of coordination and communication.

### 5.5.2 Applications of RL in Robotics

RL has a wide range of applications in robotics:

- Robotic Manipulation: RL-based robots can learn to manipulate objects, such as picking and placing items in manufacturing or logistics settings.
- Autonomous Navigation: RL enables robots to navigate autonomously in dynamic environments, including crowded spaces.
- Human-Robot Interaction: RL-based robots can be trained to interact safely and effectively with humans, facilitating tasks like collaborative assembly.
- Aerial and Underwater Robotics: RL is used in drones and underwater robots for tasks like exploration, surveillance, and environmental monitoring.

## 5.6 AI in Healthcare: Diagnostics and Drug Discovery

AI is making significant contributions to healthcare, particularly in diagnostics and drug discovery. These advanced techniques are revolutionizing medical practices and accelerating the development of new treatments.

### 5.6.1 Diagnostic Imaging

AI-powered diagnostic imaging is transforming the field of radiology:

- Medical Image Analysis: AI algorithms can analyze medical images such as X-rays, CT scans, MRIs, and pathology slides to assist radiologists in detecting diseases and abnormalities.
- Early Disease Detection: AI models can detect diseases at an early stage, improving patient outcomes. For example, they can identify early signs of cancer or neurological disorders.
- Radiomics: Radiomics involves extracting quantitative features from medical images and using AI to analyze patterns, which can provide insights into disease diagnosis, prognosis, and treatment planning.

### 5.6.2 Drug Discovery and Development

AI is revolutionizing the process of discovering and developing new drugs:

- Drug Design: AI models can predict the binding affinity between potential drug compounds and target proteins, which is crucial in designing new drugs. This process, known as virtual screening, accelerates drug discovery by identifying promising candidates more efficiently.
- Drug Repurposing: AI-driven approaches analyze existing drugs and their interactions to identify potential new uses or applications. This can lead to the discovery of treatments for diseases that were not originally intended.
- Clinical Trial Optimization: AI algorithms can analyze patient data, including genomics and clinical records, to identify suitable candidates for clinical trials and predict patient responses to different treatments. This leads to more efficient and personalized trials.
- Drug Formulation: AI is used to optimize drug formulations, ensuring that medications are effective, stable, and have desirable properties for administration.
- Chemical Synthesis: AI-driven robotic systems can automate chemical synthesis, speeding up the process of producing and testing potential drug compounds.
- Drug Safety: AI models are employed to predict potential side effects and assess the safety of drug candidates. This helps prioritize compounds with a lower risk of adverse effects.
- Regulatory Compliance: AI systems assist in navigating complex regulatory requirements for drug approval, streamlining the submission process to regulatory authorities.

### 5.6.3 Advantages and Challenges in Healthcare AI

While AI has immense potential in healthcare, it also presents certain advantages and challenges:

**Advantages** :

- Early Detection: AI can identify diseases at early stages when treatment is more effective.
- Personalized Medicine: AI enables personalized treatment plans based on patients' genetic profiles and medical history.
- Efficiency: AI streamlines processes, reducing healthcare costs and waiting times.
- Remote Monitoring: AI-powered devices allow for continuous remote monitoring of patients' health.

**Challenges:**

- Data Privacy: Handling sensitive patient data requires stringent security and privacy measures.
- Ethical Concerns: Ethical issues, such as bias in algorithms and patient consent for data use, need to be addressed.
- Regulatory Hurdles: Developing and implementing AI in healthcare must adhere to strict regulatory standards.
- Integration: Integrating AI systems with existing healthcare infrastructure can be complex.

In this chapter, we explored advanced AI techniques, including deep reinforcement learning, generative adversarial networks, natural language processing, computer vision, and AI applications in healthcare. These cutting-edge technologies are at the forefront of AI research and have the potential to transform industries and improve our quality of life. However, they also present challenges related to ethics, data privacy, and regulatory compliance that must be carefully considered and addressed as AI continues to advance. As AI technology evolves, its impact on society will become increasingly profound, shaping the way we work, live, and interact with the world around us. Understanding these advanced AI techniques and their implications is essential for staying at the forefront of this rapidly evolving field.

# Chapter 6: Implementing AI Solutions

In this chapter, we will delve into the practical aspects of implementing AI solutions. While understanding AI concepts and techniques is crucial, the true value of artificial intelligence lies in its application to real-world problems. We will explore the steps involved in planning, developing, and deploying AI solutions, as well as the challenges and considerations that come with it.

## 6.1 Planning Your AI Project

Before embarking on an AI project, careful planning is essential. The success of an AI solution depends on defining clear objectives, understanding the problem domain, and identifying the resources and data required.

### 6.1.1 Defining Objectives and Goals

The first step in any AI project is to define clear objectives and goals. What problem are you trying to solve with AI? What are the specific outcomes you hope to achieve? These objectives should be well-defined, measurable, and aligned with your organization's overall mission and strategy.

### 6.1.2 Problem Understanding and Domain Knowledge

Understanding the problem domain is critical. You need domain expertise to grasp the intricacies of the problem you're tackling. AI practitioners should collaborate closely with subject matter experts to ensure that the AI solution addresses real-world challenges effectively.

### 6.1.3 Data Assessment

Data is the lifeblood of AI. Assess the availability and quality of data relevant to your project. Is there enough data to train and validate AI models? Is the data clean and free from biases? Data preprocessing, cleaning, and augmentation may be necessary to prepare the data for AI training.

### 6.1.4 Resource Allocation

AI projects require various resources, including computing power, software tools, and skilled personnel. Allocate resources based on project complexity and scale. Consider whether you'll use cloud-based services, on-premises infrastructure, or a combination of both.

### 6.1.5 Ethical and Regulatory Considerations

Consider the ethical implications of your AI project. Ensure that your data collection and usage comply with privacy regulations and ethical guidelines. Ethical AI practices are not just a legal requirement but also a crucial aspect of maintaining public trust.

## 6.2 Data Preparation and Preprocessing

Data preparation is a significant portion of any AI project. High-quality, well-preprocessed data is essential for training accurate AI models.

### 6.2.1 Data Collection

Collecting data can involve various methods, including web scraping, sensor data acquisition, surveys, or using pre-existing datasets. Ensure that data collection practices align with privacy and consent requirements.

### 6.2.2 Data Cleaning

Data cleaning involves identifying and rectifying errors, missing values, and inconsistencies in the dataset. Cleaning is often an iterative process that ensures data accuracy.

### 6.2.3 Data Labeling

In supervised learning tasks, data labeling is crucial. This process involves annotating data instances with the correct labels, such as class labels for classification tasks or bounding boxes for object detection.

### 6.2.4 Feature Engineering

Feature engineering is the process of selecting, transforming, and creating relevant features from the data to improve model performance. It requires domain expertise and creativity to extract meaningful information from raw data.

**6.2.5 Data Splitting**

To evaluate the performance of AI models, data is typically split into training, validation, and test sets. The training set is used to train the model, the validation set helps tune hyperparameters, and the test set assesses model generalization.

## 6.3 Model Development and Training

Once data is prepared, it's time to develop and train AI models. The choice of algorithms, architecture, and training strategies depends on the nature of the problem and data.

**6.3.1 Algorithm Selection**

Select appropriate AI algorithms based on the problem type. For example, deep learning models like convolutional neural networks (CNNs) excel in image recognition, while recurrent neural networks (RNNs) are suited for sequential data.

**6.3.2 Model Architecture**

Design the architecture of your AI model. This involves defining the network structure, including the number of layers, units, and activation functions. In deep learning, architectures like ResNet, LSTM, and Transformer have been influential.

**6.3.3 Hyperparameter Tuning**

Hyperparameters are settings that control model behavior. Tuning involves selecting the right hyperparameters to optimize model performance. Techniques like grid search or random search are commonly used for this purpose.

**6.3.4 Training and Validation**

Train the model using the training data and validate its performance using the validation set. Monitor metrics like accuracy, loss, and convergence. Fine-tune the model as needed.

**6.3.5 Regularization and Optimization**

Regularization techniques like dropout and L2 regularization help prevent overfitting, where the model performs well on the training data but poorly on unseen data. Optimization algorithms like Adam or SGD fine-tune model weights during training.

## 6.4 Model Evaluation and Testing

After training, it's crucial to evaluate the model's performance thoroughly.

**6.4.1 Evaluation Metrics**

Select appropriate evaluation metrics based on the problem. For classification tasks, metrics like accuracy, precision, recall, and F1-score are commonly used. Regression tasks may use metrics like Mean Absolute Error (MAE) or Mean Squared Error (MSE).

## 6.4.2 Cross-Validation

Cross-validation is a technique to assess model performance robustly. It involves splitting the data into multiple folds, training and testing the model on different combinations of folds, and averaging the results.

## 6.4.3 Testing and Generalization

Use the test dataset to evaluate how well the model generalizes to new, unseen data. This step provides an estimate of the model's real-world performance.

## 6.5 Deployment of AI Models

Deploying AI models into production is a critical step that involves making AI capabilities accessible to end-users or applications.

### 6.5.1 Model Deployment Platforms

Choose a deployment platform that suits your project requirements. Cloud platforms like AWS, Azure, and Google Cloud offer AI services and infrastructure for deployment. Alternatively, on-premises deployment is an option for organizations with specific data security or compliance needs.

### 6.5.2 Integration with Applications

Integrate AI models into your existing applications or create new applications that leverage AI capabilities. This may involve developing APIs or microservices for model inference.

### 6.5.3 Scalability and Performance

Consider scalability and performance requirements. Ensure that the deployed model can handle the expected load and response times. Implement strategies like load balancing and auto-scaling for dynamic workloads.

### 6.5.4 Monitoring and Maintenance

Continuous monitoring of deployed AI models is essential. Monitor model performance, data drift, and concept drift. Implement maintenance procedures to update models as new data becomes available and to address issues that may arise.

## 6.6 Challenges and Considerations in AI Implementation

AI implementation is not without its challenges and considerations.

### 6.6.1 Ethical Considerations

AI systems can perpetuate biases present in training data. Implement measures to address bias and ensure fairness in AI applications, particularly in sensitive domains like finance and healthcare.

### 6.6.2 Data Security and Privacy

Protecting data is paramount. Implement robust data security measures, encryption, and access controls to safeguard sensitive information.

### 6.6.3 Regulatory Compliance

Comply with relevant regulations, such as GDPR for data privacy and HIPAA for healthcare data. Understand the legal and ethical obligations associated with your AI project and ensure that your implementation adheres to these regulations. Failure to comply with regulatory requirements can result in legal consequences and reputational damage.

### 6.6.4 Explainability and Transparency

AI models can be complex and difficult to interpret. In some cases, it's essential to provide explanations for AI-driven decisions, especially in applications where human lives or critical decisions are at stake. Ensure that your AI implementation can provide transparent and interpretable results when necessary.

### 6.6.5 Model Governance

Implement robust model governance practices. Keep records of model versions, data used, and the decisions made by AI systems. This helps in auditing, debugging, and ensuring accountability for AI-driven outcomes.

### 6.6.6 User Training and Acceptance

Users and stakeholders may need training and education to effectively utilize AI solutions. Ensure that users understand the capabilities, limitations, and potential biases of AI systems. Building trust and acceptance among users is crucial for successful AI adoption.

### 6.6.7 Cost Considerations

AI implementation can be resource-intensive. Consider the total cost of ownership, including infrastructure, personnel, maintenance, and ongoing operational expenses. Develop a clear budget and cost management plan.

### 6.6.8 Change Management

Introducing AI into an organization often requires a change in workflows and processes. Implement change management strategies to minimize disruption and help employees adapt to new AI-driven workflows.

# 6.7 Continuous Improvement

AI is not a one-time effort; it's an ongoing journey. Continuous improvement is vital for staying competitive and adapting to changing circumstances.

### 6.7.1 Model Retraining

Data drift, concept drift, and changing business conditions can impact model performance over time. Plan for periodic model retraining to keep your AI solution up-to-date and accurate.

### 6.7.2 Feedback Loops

Establish feedback loops with end-users and stakeholders. Collect feedback on the AI system's performance and use it to identify areas for improvement.

### 6.7.3 Research and Development

Stay informed about the latest advancements in AI research. Evaluate whether new techniques or models could enhance your existing AI solutions.

### 6.7.4 Benchmarking

Regularly benchmark your AI system's performance against industry standards and competitors. Benchmarking provides insights into how well your AI solution stacks up in the market.

### 6.7.5 Ethical Auditing

Periodically conduct ethical audits of your AI systems. Evaluate whether your models are causing unintended harm or reinforcing biases. Make necessary adjustments to ensure ethical AI practices.

# 6.8 Case Studies in AI Implementation

Learning from real-world case studies can provide valuable insights into AI implementation. Here are a few illustrative examples:

### 6.8.1 Healthcare Diagnostics

In healthcare, AI-powered diagnostic tools have been deployed to assist radiologists in interpreting medical images. These tools can quickly analyze X-rays, CT scans, and MRIs, helping identify anomalies and diseases with high accuracy. The implementation involves integrating AI models with existing hospital systems, ensuring compliance with medical regulations, and providing ongoing training to medical professionals.

### 6.8.2 E-Commerce Recommendation Systems

E-commerce platforms heavily rely on recommendation systems powered by AI. These systems analyze user behavior, purchase history, and product data to suggest personalized products to customers. AI implementation in e-commerce involves collecting and processing vast amounts of customer data, training recommendation algorithms, and optimizing the user experience.

### 6.8.3 Autonomous Vehicles

The deployment of AI in autonomous vehicles involves a complex integration of sensors, perception algorithms, and decision-making systems. These vehicles must adhere to stringent safety and regulatory standards. The implementation process includes rigorous testing, validation, and real-world trials to ensure the vehicles can operate safely in diverse environments.

### 6.8.4 Fraud Detection in Finance

Financial institutions utilize AI to detect fraudulent activities in real-time. AI models analyze transaction data, user behavior, and historical fraud patterns to identify suspicious transactions. Implementation requires robust security measures to protect sensitive financial data and continuous model monitoring to adapt to evolving fraud tactics.

Implementing AI solutions is a multifaceted process that requires careful planning, data preparation, model development, and deployment. It also involves addressing ethical, regulatory, and operational challenges. Successful AI implementation brings tangible benefits, such as improved decision-making, increased efficiency, and enhanced customer experiences. However, it is crucial to approach AI implementation as an ongoing endeavor, continuously evolving and improving to meet changing needs and expectations. By embracing the principles outlined in this chapter and learning from real-world case studies, organizations can harness the power of AI to drive innovation and achieve their strategic goals.

# Chapter 7: AI in Society and Ethics

In this chapter, we explore the profound impact of artificial intelligence (AI) on society and delve into the ethical considerations that arise as AI technologies become increasingly integrated into our lives. From automation and the future of work to bias and transparency, this chapter explores the complex web of societal challenges and opportunities that AI presents.

# 7.1 The AI Revolution: Transforming Industries and Workforce

The AI revolution is reshaping industries and the workforce, bringing both opportunities and challenges. Understanding the dynamics of this transformation is crucial for individuals, organizations, and policymakers.

### 7.1.1 Automation and Job Displacement

AI-driven automation has the potential to disrupt traditional job roles across various industries. Routine, repetitive tasks are increasingly being automated, leading to concerns about job displacement. However, AI also creates new job opportunities in areas such as AI development, data science, and AI ethics.

### 7.1.2 Upskilling and Reskilling

To adapt to the changing job landscape, individuals and organizations must prioritize upskilling and reskilling. Lifelong learning becomes essential, and educational institutions and employers play a vital role in providing relevant training and resources.

### 7.1.3 Human-AI Collaboration

Rather than a complete replacement of human labor, AI often serves as a tool to augment human capabilities. Human-AI collaboration can enhance productivity and decision-making, emphasizing the importance of human skills like creativity, critical thinking, and emotional intelligence.

## 7.2 Ethical Considerations in AI Development

Ethical considerations are central to AI development. As AI systems make autonomous decisions and influence various aspects of society, addressing ethical concerns is imperative.

### 7.2.1 Bias and Fairness

Bias in AI systems, often stemming from biased training data, can lead to discriminatory outcomes. Ensuring fairness in AI, especially in sensitive applications like hiring and lending, requires proactive measures to detect and mitigate bias.

### 7.2.2 Transparency and Explainability

AI systems can be complex and opaque, making it difficult to understand their decision-making processes. Transparency and explainability mechanisms are essential for ensuring accountability and trust. Techniques like model interpretability and explainable AI (XAI) aim to shed light on AI decision logic.

### 7.2.3 Privacy and Data Security

AI relies on vast amounts of data, raising concerns about privacy and data security. Protecting individuals' data rights and implementing robust security measures are fundamental ethical considerations in AI development.

### 7.2.4 Accountability and Responsibility

Determining accountability for AI decisions is a challenging ethical issue. When AI systems make errors or cause harm, defining who is responsible and liable becomes crucial. Legal and regulatory frameworks must evolve to address these challenges.

### 7.3 AI in Healthcare: Balancing Innovation and Ethics

AI is revolutionizing healthcare, offering advanced diagnostic and treatment options. However, ethical considerations are paramount in the highly sensitive healthcare domain.

#### 7.3.1 Diagnostic Accuracy and Accountability

AI-based diagnostic tools, while highly accurate, must be used responsibly. Errors in healthcare AI can have life-altering consequences, necessitating robust validation and accountability mechanisms.

#### 7.3.2 Privacy and Patient Consent

Collecting and analyzing patient data for AI-driven healthcare solutions requires strict adherence to privacy regulations and obtaining informed patient consent. Ethical data practices are essential to maintain patient trust.

#### 7.3.3 Equity in Healthcare Access

AI has the potential to improve healthcare access, especially in underserved areas. However, ensuring equitable access to AI-driven healthcare solutions is an ethical imperative. Disparities in access and affordability must be addressed.

#### 7.3.4 Ethical AI in Medical Research

AI accelerates medical research and drug discovery. Ethical considerations in AI-powered research include data sharing, informed consent, and responsible experimentation.

## 7.4 AI in Education: Enhancing Learning and Equity

AI is transforming education by personalizing learning experiences and improving educational outcomes. However, ethical considerations are vital to ensure equitable access and protect student data.

#### 7.4.1 Personalization and Privacy

AI-driven personalized learning can enhance student engagement and outcomes. However, it requires the responsible handling of student data to protect privacy and security.

#### 7.4.2 Addressing Educational Disparities

AI has the potential to bridge educational disparities by providing tailored support to students with diverse learning needs. Ensuring that AI-driven educational resources are accessible to all students is an ethical imperative.

#### 7.4.3 Ethical AI Tutoring Systems

AI-powered tutoring systems can provide valuable support to students. However, ethical tutoring systems should prioritize the well-being of students, avoid harmful biases, and respect cultural and individual differences.

### 7.4.4 AI in Assessment and Grading

AI is used for automated assessment and grading. Ethical concerns include the transparency of grading algorithms and ensuring that AI assessments are free from bias.

## 7.5 AI in Criminal Justice: Balancing Efficiency and Fairness

AI is increasingly employed in criminal justice systems, from predictive policing to parole decisions. Balancing efficiency with fairness and justice is a critical ethical challenge .

### 7.5.1 Predictive Policing and Bias

Predictive policing algorithms can perpetuate biases present in historical crime data. Addressing bias and ensuring fairness in law enforcement AI systems is essential.

### 7.5.2 Risk Assessment in Criminal Justice

AI is used to assess the risk of recidivism and make parole or sentencing recommendations. Ethical considerations include transparency, accountability, and avoiding discriminatory outcomes.

### 7.5.3 Facial Recognition and Privacy

The use of facial recognition technology in criminal justice has privacy and surveillance implications. Ethical guidelines must govern its use to protect individuals' rights.

### 7.5.4 Accountability in AI-Assisted Policing

Accountability mechanisms are essential when AI systems are used in policing. Ensuring transparency and oversight is crucial to prevent misuse and protect civil liberties.

## 7.6 AI and Bias: Addressing Unintended Discrimination

Bias in AI systems, whether in hiring, lending, or criminal justice, is a significant ethical concern. Addressing bias requires a combination of technical and ethical solutions.

### 7.6.1 Sources of Bias

Bias in AI can originate from biased training data, biased algorithms, or biased human decision-making. Identifying and mitigating these sources is essential.

### 7.6.2 Fairness-Aware AI

Fairness-aware AI techniques aim to detect and mitigate bias in AI systems. Approaches like reweighting training data, adversarial debiasing, and fairness constraints can help promote fair outcomes.

### 7.6.3 Auditing AI for Bias

Regular audits of AI systems for bias are crucial. These audits involve evaluating system performance across different demographic groups and taking corrective actions when bias is detected.

### 7.6.4 Diversity in AI Development

Promoting diversity in AI development teams isessential for addressing bias and ensuring that AI systems are designed with a wide range of perspectives. Diverse teams can better recognize and mitigate potential sources of bias and discrimination.

## 7.7 AI in Governance and Policy

Governments and policymakers play a pivotal role in shaping the ethical and regulatory landscape of AI. Balancing innovation with responsible AI governance is a complex challenge.

### 7.7.1 Developing AI Regulations

Governments worldwide are working to establish regulations and guidelines for AI. These regulations encompass areas such as data privacy, algorithmic transparency, and liability frameworks.

### 7.7.2 Ethical AI Principles

Ethical AI principles serve as a foundation for responsible AI development and deployment. These principles often include fairness, transparency, accountability, and respect for human rights.

### 7.7.3 International Collaboration

AI is a global phenomenon, and international collaboration is essential to address ethical and regulatory challenges. Collaborative efforts can help create consistent standards and promote responsible AI adoption worldwide.

### 7.7.4 Ethical Considerations in AI Research

Ethical considerations extend to AI research itself. Researchers must consider the potential societal impacts of their work and prioritize responsible AI development.

## 7.8 The Future of AI Ethics

The field of AI ethics continues to evolve as AI technologies advance and their societal implications become more apparent. Anticipating future ethical challenges is essential for proactive ethical AI development.

### 7.8.1 Ethical Considerations in Advanced AI Systems

As AI systems become more sophisticated, ethical considerations become increasingly complex. Issues related to superintelligent AI, autonomous weapons, and AI in brain-computer interfaces require careful ethical scrutiny.

### 7.8.2 Human Rights and AI

AI technologies should respect and uphold human rights, including privacy, freedom of expression, and non-discrimination. Ensuring that AI aligns with these fundamental rights is an ongoing challenge.

### 7.8.3 AI and Environmental Sustainability

AI has the potential to contribute to environmental sustainability by optimizing energy consumption and addressing climate-related challenges. Ethical considerations include the responsible use of AI to address environmental issues.

### 7.8.4 Evolving Ethical Frameworks

Ethical frameworks for AI are likely to evolve over time. Stakeholders, including governments, industry leaders, and civil society, will shape these frameworks to address emerging challenges and opportunities.

AI's impact on society and ethics is profound, touching nearly every aspect of our lives. While AI offers tremendous potential for innovation, efficiency, and improved quality of life, it also raises complex ethical considerations. These considerations encompass fairness, transparency, accountability, privacy, and more.

To navigate the ethical landscape of AI successfully, individuals, organizations, governments, and researchers must work collaboratively. Responsible AI development and deployment require continuous vigilance, adaptability, and a commitment to upholding fundamental ethical principles.

As AI technologies continue to advance, so too must our understanding of the ethical challenges they pose. The future of AI ethics will be shaped by our ability to anticipate, address, and adapt to the evolving societal, technological, and ethical landscape. In this rapidly changing AI-driven world, ethical considerations remain at the forefront of the AI revolution, guiding us towards a future where AI benefits all of humanity.

www.ingramcontent.com/pod-product-compliance
Lightning Source LLC
Chambersburg PA
CBHW051402250726
48656CB00006B/2237